THE IMPACT OF POST-9/11 VISA POLICIES ON TRAVEL TO THE UNITED STATES

Brent Neiman
Harvard University

Phillip Swagel
Department of the Treasury

June 2007

THE IMPACT OF POST-9/11 VISA POLICIES
ON TRAVEL TO THE UNITED STATES

Brent Neiman
Harvard University

Phillip Swagel
Department of the Treasury

June 2007

This paper examines the impact of post-9/11 changes in visa and security policy on business and leisure travel to the United States. American businesses, tourism industry representatives, and politicians pointed to changes in visa policies as being responsible for a sharp decline in short-term visitors following the September 11 attacks. Several foreign governments likewise complained that visa requirements and other security measures were making it difficult for their citizens to travel to the United States. Using an empirical model which distinguishes the impact of visa policy from economic and country-specific factors, we find that changes in visa policy in the aftermath of 9/11 were not important contributors to the decrease in travel to the United States. Rather, the reduction in entries was largest among travelers who were not required to obtain a visa.

The views and opinions expressed in this paper are those of the authors and do not necessarily represent official Treasury positions or policy. We thank Effi Benmelech, Scott Carrell, Karen Dynan, Richard Falkenrath, Judith Hellerstein, Larry Katz, Ilyana Kuziemko, David Meyer, Harvey Rosen, and seminar participants at the NBER Working Group on the Economics of National Security for helpful discussions and comments. Cindy Soo provided excellent research assistance.

1 Introduction

The number of business and leisure travelers arriving in the United States dropped sharply following the terror attacks of September 11, 2001. The number of non-immigrant visitors fell by more than 17 percent for the period October 2002 to September 2003 (the government's fiscal year 2003) compared to the number of visitors in fiscal year 2000, and travel to the United States had not recovered by late 2005 (Figure 1). In contrast, the number of legal permanent immigrants did not change appreciably, though illegal immigration is believed to have declined after 9/11 in response to heightened security measures.[1] This paper examines whether changes in visa policy, which applied only to visitors from certain countries, were the key contributors to the decline in short-term travel to the United States, or whether economic, psychological, or other factors such as more stringent airport security had a larger impact on travel. Our results do not apply to foreigners seeking to work or study in the United States, because the data do not include longer-term arrivals such as students.

In the wake of the attacks, the U.S. government enhanced a wide range of border security policies. Steps taken included both visible changes in security procedures at airports and other entry points that affect all visitors, as well as changes in policies governing visa issuance that affect only travelers who require a visa to enter the United States. The changes in visa policy were not surprising in the wake of the attacks, given that the 9/11 terrorists had entered the United States with legitimate visas.

Commentators in both the public and private sectors have claimed that tougher visa policies are an important factor behind the decline in travel to the United States, and express concern that post-9/11 visa policies hurt businesses by straining relationships with customers and hindering opportunities for new business. For example, a recent Bloomberg article on the decline in business travel to the United States after 9/11 referenced an estimate by the National Foreign Trade Council that tougher entry rules cost U.S. businesses $31 billion from 2002 to 2004 (the article was also published by the *International Herald Tribune* under the title "'Fortress America' visa system scaring businesses away.")[2] In late 2006, the *London Times* estimated the cost of the decline in foreign tourists coming to the United States since 9/11 at $286 billion.[3] The article ties a large share of this cost to visa policy when it states, "The question is why America is missing out. The immediate obstacle is the stricter security introduced since September 2001."

Suggestions that changes in visa policy played a fundamental role in the immediate post-9/11 decline in foreign visitors also can be found on the web sites and in the press releases of organizations ranging from think tanks to lobbyists. In December 2006, Tom Ridge, the first Secretary of Homeland Security, was involved with a report from a travel industry group that suggests, among other things, that the United States reassess the current visa and border control regime.[4]

The issue has also garnered attention from policymakers. A Federal Reserve Bank of Dallas publication highlights companies' concerns about the new post-9/11 visa requirements (Orrenius 2003). The House of Representatives Government Reform Committee held hearings on the topic in 2006, where even cello virtuoso Yo-Yo Ma chimed in, testifying that visa policies were stifling cultural interchange. Foreign officials similarly have voiced complaints about post-9/11 changes in visa policy.

---

[1] Passel (2005) estimates that about 700,000 unauthorized immigrants entered the United States per year during 2000-2004, compared with 750,000 per year during 1995-1999.
[2] Bliss and Hughes, "World's 'Worst' Visa System Scares Business Away from U.S.", December 25, 2006, Bloomberg.com.
[3] "Tourism Slump Worries U.S.", The Sunday Times – Business, September 17, 2006.
[4] Waterman, "Ridge Proposes U.S. Visa Reforms", United Press International, December 22, 2006.

This paper assesses the impact of the post-9/11 visa regime on non-immigrant entries to the United States. Our motivation is as follows. The changes in the visa regime were undertaken for the purposes of national security. We take this benefit as given and will not seek to measure it. As detailed above, however, many people weigh this potential benefit against the perceived cost that changes in visa policy played an important role in the decline in temporary visitors to the United States. Our goal is to introduce empirical evidence suggesting the scale of this cost.

We are aware of no recent economic analysis in the research literature that examines the impact of economic, geopolitical, and security-related factors on business and leisure travel.[5] To distinguish the effects of visa policy from other factors such as more general security measures and the psychological impact of the attacks, we compare the impact of the 9/11 attacks on travel by visitors that require a visa to enter the United States with the impact on visitors who do not. To do this, we group countries by their participation in the visa waiver program, a section of the U.S. legal code under which citizens of 27 countries (as of early 2007) are allowed to visit the United States temporarily without first obtaining a visa. The countries included in the visa waiver program are those whose citizens are deemed unlikely to pose a security threat and are expected to leave the United States in line with immigration rules (Table 1). In 2003, entries under this program represented roughly half of all overseas visitors to the United States (Siskin, 2004).

All travelers are subject to routine security restrictions such as examination of their passports and luggage upon arrival into the United States, but only visitors from countries that do not participate in the visa waiver program are affected by changes in non-immigrant visa policy. Our econometric approach is based on this distinction: some changes in overall security policy after 9/11 applied to all visitors to the United States, but changes in visa policy applied only to certain travelers. The difference in treatment between travelers who must obtain a visa and those who can enter without one provides a policy-induced variation by which to assess the impact of changes in the visa regime that took place in the wake of the 9/11 attacks.

The analysis suggests that stricter visa policy did not play a direct role in reducing travel to the United States in the two years following the September 11 attacks. After taking into account economic and geopolitical effects, entries from countries requiring a visa did not fall by more after 9/11 than visits by people not needing a visa. In fact, in the vast majority of our specifications, the results indicate just the opposite – the decline was largest for travelers from visa waiver countries whose citizens do not require a visa to enter the United States.[6]

Several factors could explain the large decline in travel by visitors who did not require a visa. One possibility is that the 9/11 attacks had a greater psychological effect on citizens of countries in the visa waiver program, leaving them even more reluctant to travel to the United States than citizens of other countries. Another possibility is that the heightened security screening and other burdensome informal barriers that contribute to the "hassle factor" of travel represented a proportionately larger incremental aggravation for travelers who did not require a visa, resulting in a larger reduction in entries from these countries. Under this view, people asserting that travelers requiring a visa were materially impacted by new obstacles after 9/11 might have been correct, but what they could not see was that travelers who did not require a visa, such as nationals of France or the UK, were now being scrutinized as well. Since British and French nationals received little scrutiny and suffered little aggravation before 9/11, the

---

[5] There is a large literature on the economic influences of permanent immigration patterns. We also note that Orrenius (2003) analyzes related issues for a general audience outside of a research framework.
[6] We emphasize that our conclusion that visa policy was not the primary cause of reduced non-immigrant entries does not apply to foreigners coming to the United States on worker or student visas. The factors behind a decision to work or study abroad are likely to differ markedly from influences on business and leisure travel decisions. Moreover, these visitors are not short-term and hence are generally excluded from our data. We thus provide no evidence on this issue in either direction.

relatively greater change in treatment might thus be connected to the larger impact in their travel to the United States.

In sum, after taking into account economic and country-specific factors, the post-9/11 drop in entries was at least as large among travelers who did not need a visa, and in many specifications, significantly larger. This indicates that changes in the formal visa process do not explain very much of the decline in travel to the United States. What mattered instead were either changes in foreign attitudes or changes in the post-9/11 security regime that affected the decisions of all tourists and businesspersons considering travel to the United States, not just those required to obtain visas.

2   Border Security Policy

Airport security changed substantially following 9/11, with passengers arriving in the United States facing much greater scrutiny than before the attacks. Airlines are required to send passenger lists in advance, exclusion lists are more vigorously maintained, and non-citizens are required to provide digital fingerprints and have their photograph taken on arrival. Visa approval takes longer.

State Department spokespersons have stated, however, that refusal rates did not change significantly in the wake of the attacks. Indeed, though the refusal rate reached 35.1 percent in fiscal year 2002 (following the attacks), the 31.7 percent rejection rate in fiscal year 2003 was actually below the rate during fiscal 2001, the year ending in September 2001 (Clemens 2004).[7] These slight variations in visa rejection rates explain only a small portion of the 17 percent drop in the total number of entries: the modestly higher rejection rate meant that several hundred thousand more visa applications were refused in the year after the attack than in the year before it, but the total number of entries fell by several million. Of course, it could be the case that potential visa applicants, aware of the increased scrutiny they receive in the post-9/11 world, self-select in a way that reduces the number of rejections made at U.S. diplomatic missions.

Independent from the criteria for granting or rejecting a visa application, potential travelers requiring a visa are also affected by changes in consular procedures and higher fees that make the visa process more arduous and expensive. Further, other security procedures affect all visitors, regardless of whether or not they need a visa, such as the heightened airport security and more involved screening for U.S.-bound flights that make travel less pleasant. Raising the cost of boarding a plane and obtaining a visa would be expected, on the margin, to discourage foreigners from undertaking business or leisure travel to the United States.

While some of the changes in visa policy are easily identifiable and were implemented on a specific date, others have not been publicly disclosed or were implemented over time, including being applied differently in different regions. Many of the changes, however, were instituted shortly after the terrorist attacks. A State Department report notes that "the post-September 11, 2001 era witnessed immediate efforts to effect dramatic changes in CA's [Consular Affairs] direction of the visa process" (Office of the Inspector General, Department of State 2004).

The most obvious change is that foreigners now pay more to apply for a visa to visit the United States. Visa fees rose from $45 before September 11 to $65 in June 2002 and to $100 in November 2002 (Rose 2004). Further, the time it takes to get approved for a visa increased for many applicants. Shortly after the attacks, the Department of Justice requested that two new name check procedures be added to the visa application process, requiring 20 and 30 days each. The 30-day check under the so-called "Visa Condor" program applies to visa applicants from a list of countries that is classified for national security reasons (GAO 2002). In early 2002,

---

[7] These rates exclude some small visa categories, but the pattern remains essentially identical if these are added,

American consulates began to collect a supplemental application form from male visa applicants aged 16 to 45 from every country. Visa applicants from certain countries must now undergo an in-person interview at a U.S. embassy or consulate to obtain a visa.

These changes in visa policy, however, do not impact visitors from all foreign countries because some visitors do not require a visa in the first place. The Immigration Reform and Control Act of 1986 created the Visa Waiver Program to facilitate the entry of temporary visitors from countries whose citizens were perceived as particularly unlikely to threaten U.S. national security. Under the program, foreign nationals from participating countries (listed in Table 1) are able to enter the United States for up to 90 days without obtaining a visa (nations participating in the visa waiver program must extend reciprocal treatment to Americans). Visitors are still checked against an exclusion list and must provide proof of a return ticket out of the United States and adequate financial resources for their stay. A small number of visitors from visa-waiver countries are required to obtain non-immigrant visas (for example, travelers wishing to stay in the United States on a temporary basis for more than 90 days, visitors with criminal backgrounds, and anyone who was previously denied a visa), and occasionally foreigners unaware of their eligibility for the visa waiver program will unnecessarily apply for a visa. These travelers, however, account for less than 10 percent of the non-immigrant entries from most visa waiver countries in recent years. Based on this, we assume in the regression analysis that all visitors from visa-waiver countries are without a visa, while all entrants who are citizens of countries not included in the visa waiver program require one.

Countries were added to the visa waiver program starting with the United Kingdom in 1986 and most recently with Portugal, Singapore, and Uruguay in 1999. The program was made

---

rising through FY2002, but then falling in FY2003 to below pre-9/11 levels.

permanent in 2000 and at that time included 29 countries. Argentina and Uruguay were removed from the program in 2002 and 2003, respectively.

The visa waiver program has come under review in the wake of the 9/11 attacks and subsequent incidents, as concerns have arisen that terrorists or other criminals could exploit the program. After all, Zacarias Moussaoui, a French national convicted as a co-conspirator in the September 11 attacks and Richard Reid, a British citizen convicted of trying to detonate a bomb concealed in his shoes while on a flight to the United States, both entered the United States under the Visa Waiver Program. To date, however, the program has not been changed, though efforts to improve the list of foreign nationals ineligible for entry to the United States might be seen as an attempt to address the potential vulnerability.

3   Influences on Business and Leisure Travel

A change in visa policy was only one of several factors affecting foreign travel to the United States. The September 11 attacks had a significant impact in reducing airplane travel to the United States that was independent of economic factors and security measures; one might term this a "psychological" impact in making people reluctant to fly in the immediate aftermath of the attacks. This is mirrored by the reduction in domestic U.S. air travel after 9/11: according to Department of Transportation data, the number of passengers on domestic non-stop segments in the United States was 11 percent lower in fiscal 2002 than in fiscal 2000 (Figure 2).

Economic factors affect travel as well. Strong U.S. growth would likely increase business opportunities that cause foreign businesspersons to travel to the United States, and the economic strength or weakness in travelers' home countries might similarly affect business and leisure travel. Exchange rate fluctuations change the effective cost, denominated in foreign consumption units, for foreigners considering travel to the United States. Finally, the onset of the war in Iraq appears to have led to a drop-off in travel in early 2003 as potential visitors awaited the outcome of the conflict.

There has been limited research on the economic factors that influence business and leisure travel. The most closely related studies examine the determinants of total spending by international tourists, which equals the product of the number of visits (our focus) and the average amount spent on each visit. Rhomberg and Boissonneault (1964) and Gray (1966) estimate elasticities of demand for spending by international travelers with respect to national and per capita income and exchange rates and find that the response of spending to these factors is statistically significant. Gray also finds that the cost of transportation was not a significant factor influencing international travel, though of course this and the other results could have changed in the intervening four decades. Kwack (1971) likewise shows that spending abroad by travelers responds substantially to changes in national incomes and real exchange rates and finds that these elasticities are higher for foreign travelers entering the United States than for U.S. travelers visiting foreign countries (though, again, these results apply to data from the 1960's). More recently, Di Matteo (1993) and Vilasuso and Menz (1998) find that national income and the exchange rate are the key determinants of spending by Canadians traveling in the United States.

An analytic framework to assess the influences on the number of business and pleasure travelers would model the choice of individuals of whether or not to travel to the United States, with this decision influenced by personal circumstances, including both financial and otherwise. Since the requirement of individual-level data on potential travelers is unrealistic, we estimate instead a macroeconomic framework in which the dependent variable is the monthly number of entries to the United States from individual countries of origin. The explanatory variables are economic factors such as overall GDP growth in the United States and each partner nation and changes in the real exchange rate between the two countries. We also take into account influences on travel patterns such as the season in the United States (the hemisphere of the origin country turns out not to matter), the war in Iraq, and whether a traveler requires a visa to visit the United States.

The econometric analysis is carried out on a panel of entries into the United States from each of up to 65 countries, denoted as i. This is akin to using data on bilateral trade between the United States and various partners. Country fixed effects are included to capture country-specific factors, while monthly fixed effects capture common factors that change over time. The specification includes a post-9/11 dummy variable, a dummy to indicate whether travelers from each country are eligible for the visa waiver program (VWP), and the interaction between the 9/11 and the visa waiver indicators. This allows for a "differences-in-differences" framework to assess whether post-9/11 changes affected entrants from VWP and non-VWP countries differently: all travelers to the United States were affected by the post-9/11 environment and by some changes in security procedures, but only travelers from non-VWP countries were affected by changes in visa rules. The empirical specification allows us to assess whether changes in travel patterns after 9/11 differed between travelers who needed a visa and those who did not.

4   Data and Specification

Monthly data on non-immigrant entries to the United States were obtained from the U.S. Department of Homeland Security (DHS). The data include I-94 admissions only, meaning it excludes the majority of short-term land-border admissions from Canada and Mexico. We follow DHS in focusing on these data because the large number of Canadian and Mexican entries would swamp non-immigration trends from the rest of the world that are more relevant to visa policy. Further, the motivating factors for crossing a land border may differ from the factors behind longer-distance travel of nationals beyond the immediate U.S. neighbors.

These unpublished data are compiled by DHS's Office of Immigration Statistics and include the monthly number of entries for fiscal years 1996 and 1998 to 2003 (as an example, fiscal year 2003 runs from October 2002 to September 2003).[8] There are some gaps in the data, with only annual figures available for 1995 and no data at all for 1997. We have not been able to obtain monthly data for years after 2003. The data include the number of entries by class of admission (e.g. tourist or businessperson) and by country of citizenship.[9] This last classification means that, for example, a French national arriving in the United States is counted as French regardless of whether he or she resides in France and regardless of the port of embarkation.

The number of entries consistently trended upward from the early 1990s until September 2001. After the post-9/11 drop-off, travel to the United States slowly grew back to near its former peak. Non-immigrant travel had not reached its pre-9/11 level by the end of September 2005, the most recent year for which we have data (that is, DHS has published the total number of entries for fiscal years 2004 and 2005, but has not made available monthly data by country). The panel unit root test of Im, Pesaran, and Shin (2003) rejects the null of non-stationarity for both the levels and log of entries when all countries are pooled together for the years in which continuous data are available from October 1997 to September 2003 (the null is rejected with and without including a trend in the test).

We drop countries lacking economic data such as measures of output and inflation on at least a quarterly frequency. The resulting sample includes 65 countries and covers over 86 percent of all entries in fiscal year 2003. Our sample contains 23 countries that were participants at some point in the visa waiver program – a few countries move in or out of the visa waiver

---

[8] Most of these data have been aggregated into annual statistics and included in the Office of Immigration Statistics' *Yearbook of Immigration Statistics*, but the monthly statistics on country-by-country entries are not published separately (the unpublished data we use are from DHS Table 607).
[9] The split between business and pleasure is not always available and in some cases is imputed, preventing us from further including these characteristics in our analysis.

program during the years in our sample.[10] We have tested our results with a constant panel, omitting these countries as well as others that enter the data set after 1995. Though this procedure requires omitting a large number of observations, it has little qualitative impact on our results.

We further exclude three countries from our primary specifications, though we report full results with their inclusion in the appendix. First, we exclude Argentina because the very close timing of its economic and political crisis, its removal from the visa waiver program, and the 9/11 attacks potentially poses problems for our identification strategy. We also exclude Canadian and Mexican entrants because our I-94 data excludes land-border crossings and hence captures only the small share of entrants from those nations who arrive from another country or via air travel. Further, the number of Mexican visitors requiring visas is extremely large relative to the number of other entries that require visas, so it has the potential to swamp developments in other countries. In Appendix Table A1, we provide results for the cases when all countries are included, when only Argentina is removed, and when only Canada and Mexico are removed. Our basic results holds for all of these cases. When including Canada, we consider it along with the visa waiver countries, even though this is not formally the case, because nearly all Canadians enter the United States without a visa under a different agreement than the visa waiver program.

The data indicate that both international travel to the United States and domestic travel within the United States declined considerably following the 9/11 attacks (Figures 1 and 2).[11] The recovery of domestic travel, however, was far more rapid and steady, suggesting the possibility of different influences on international travelers. The total number of entries in the

---

[10] Argentina was removed, while Australia, Slovenia, Portugal, and Singapore were added.

[11] There is a very strong cyclical component to monthly travel data. Graphs such as Figure 1, Panel B, that are labeled "seasonally adjusted" have had monthly variation stripped out by adjusting the raw series by the coefficients from regressions of the log series on month dummies. The short time series involved, however, mean that this

aggregate data from all 204 countries declined by more than 17 percent from the last full fiscal year before the attacks to fiscal 2003 (Figure 1). Table 2 shows that the corresponding drop in entries from our sample of 65 countries is also 17 percent. This includes a 22 percent decline in entries over this period from the 23 visa waiver countries in our sample, and an 11 percent drop in entries from non-visa waiver countries.[12]

Our sample of countries includes a very high percentage of entries from visa waiver countries, which implies that the 22 percent drop in entries from these countries in our data is close to the decline in the aggregate data for all visa waiver countries (that is, including countries not in our sample). Coupled with the facts that aggregate entries dropped 17 percent and that entries from visa waiver countries accounted for about 55 percent of all entries over this period, this implies the aggregate drop from all non-visa waiver countries was about 11 percent—the same as in our sample. This suggests that our dataset is representative of entries from both visa waiver and non-visa waiver countries.

The summary statistics in Table 2, both for the aggregate data as well as for the countries in our dataset, do not indicate that visa policies contributed substantially to the drop in entries; indeed, the raw numbers suggest the opposite in that the average decline was larger for entries from countries whose citizens did not require a visa. Figure 3 plots seasonally adjusted entry data from a constant panel of all countries whose visa-waiver program status did not change from 1996 on (including those for which we have no economic data). The figure indicates that both the trend growth before 9/11 and the subsequent response to the attacks is remarkably similar from citizens of the two groups of countries. If anything, travel from countries not

procedure is highly imperfect. Small or short term fluctuations or correlations in fluctuations should not be taken too seriously.

[12] As discussed above, we exclude Argentina, Canada, and Mexico from our baseline regressions, and so have also excluded them in these calculations. Given Mexico's small increase in travelers, including these countries would make the relative drop in visa waiver entries even larger.

requiring visas exhibit the more significant negative response. Hence, just from looking at these data, one might conclude that the reduction in business and pleasure travel resulted from the psychological or economic effects of the terrorist attacks that were common to all countries, or from general security measures impacting all travelers rather than from changes in visa policy. While the summary statistics suggest that the impact of visa policies on non-immigrant entries was limited, a multivariate regression framework is required to distinguish the influence of visa policies from economic and other factors impacting travel decisions.

Our base specification for entries from country i in month t takes the form:

$$\ln(Entries_{it}) = \beta_1 Country_i + \beta_2 Time_t + \psi \begin{bmatrix} VWP \\ \Delta \ln GDP \\ \Delta \ln RER \end{bmatrix}_{it} + \beta_3 (VWP * Post\text{-}9/11)_{it} + \varepsilon_{it} \qquad (1)$$

where we include country and time dummy variables. Data on real GDP, inflation, and nominal exchange rates in terms of local currency per dollar are from the IMF's International Financial Statistics (IFS) database. The economic and indicator variables are at a monthly frequency; for real GDP, we linearly interpolated quarterly data to obtain monthly values.[13] The real exchange rate, RER, is calculated using the nominal exchange rate (in foreign currency per dollar) and U.S. and foreign consumer price inflation; a larger value thus represents a real appreciation of the U.S. dollar. Real GDP growth and the real exchange rate are included as 12-month growth rates. The VWP variable is one for countries participating in the visa waiver program and zero otherwise. Since the specification includes country fixed effects, the VWP coefficient by itself is estimated entirely from time series variation in countries that transition in or out of the program.

The specification uses the log of the number of entries along with country fixed effects, so it matches changes in entrants in percentage terms against changes in economic variables, also in percentage terms. As such, the coefficients on economic variables provide easily interpreted elasticities. Time dummies capture changes in aggregate entries from one period to the next.

Estimating with the log of entries is somewhat problematic, however, in that it gives the same weight in the regression to a 10 percent change in visits from a country with many travelers such as Japan as it does a 10 percent change in visits from a country with relatively few entries such as Kazakhstan. Since our goal is to understand the relationship between changes in visa policy and the number of non-immigrant entrants to the United States, in our baseline specification we weight the regressions by the level of entrants for each country in fiscal 1996.[14] This approach makes sense when one is concerned about heterogeneity in the true underlying relationships across countries and wants to put more weight on the estimated relationships for the larger countries (that is, to give more weight to the GDP elasticity of visits for Japan than for Kazakhstan).

It is also interesting, however, to consider the case without weights, which makes sense if one believes the source of error in the estimates is a country-month specific unobservable shocks; the unweighted regression treats each observation as yielding the same amount of information about the impact on visa policies. We see the weighted regressions as more relevant to this analysis, but report both weighted and unweighted results for all specifications. Finally, in Appendix Table A2, we also consider alternative weighting schemes -- population, PPP-adjusted per capita GDP levels, and bilateral trade with the U.S. in 1995. These weighting schemes are broadly consistent with our results in that none of the interaction coefficients are positive and significant at 5% or better. We prefer the baseline weights, however, because each

---

[13] The consumer price index for Australia is available only by quarters in some years and is linearly interpolated to obtain monthly values.

[14] Using weights that are in any way related to the independent variable can be problematic, particularly if there is a time-series element to the weights that allows them to be correlated to the error term in the regressions. Here, we

of these alternatives greatly skews countries relative to their import to U.S. tourism. For instance, India and Singapore have disproportionately large impacts on the population and per-capita GDP weighted regressions, respectively.

In all of the regressions, we assume that the causality runs from macroeconomic variables of GDP growth and the exchange rate to the number of entries, and that the number of visits from any one country is not large enough to affect aggregate growth rates or currency markets. This is based on the observation that even the high water mark of roughly 3.5 million temporary visits from all countries in July 2000 is modest compared to the U.S. population or labor force, and that the spending of these visitors and thus their impact on the exchange value of the dollar is dwarfed by the trillions of dollars in daily turnover in foreign exchange markets.

The coefficient on the interaction of the post-9/11 and VWP indicators measures the differential impact of 9/11 on people from visa waiver countries compared to visitors who must obtain a visa. A significant positive value on this interaction term would indicate that, conditional on the economic factors and other controls, post-9/11 changes were associated with a larger reduction in entries from non-visa waiver countries than visa waiver countries. Indeed, proponents of the "tough visa hypothesis" would predict a quantitatively large and statistically significant coefficient on this interaction, suggesting stricter visa policies applying only to non-VWP entries greatly affected the level of entries. In fact, the vast majority of our results generate a negative coefficient on this interaction term, suggesting the decline in travel to the United States after 9/11 was at least as pronounced in countries whose citizens did not require a visa. This negative coefficient is statistically significant in many specifications, including both weighted and unweighted regressions.

---

worry less about this because our data is in percent changes at a monthly frequency, and hence the error term is unlikely to be correlated to the weights, which are the levels of entrants in only the first year of our dataset.

To be sure, we do not interpret this negative coefficient to mean that stricter visa policy led to increased entries from affected countries—it is not reasonable to believe that the demand for travel increases when it becomes more costly. Rather, we are suggesting that the factors behind the decline in visits to the United States were either unrelated or negatively correlated to the tightening in visa policies after September 11.

5   Regression Results

The first half of Table 3 provides results from our baseline specification panel regression (1) on the influences of the number of entries to the United States. Column (1) shows the baseline specification in which we weight by a previous annual level of entries, and column (2) shows the identical specification with no weighting. In addition, we include results for specifications that include country-specific linear trends in columns (3) and (4). We consider these specifications less meaningful, since the overall pattern of entries shown in Figure 3 does not suggest important differences between the groups in terms of long-term trends and the limited time series is not sufficient to precisely estimate a stable differential trend between the two groups of countries. Further, since countries appear in our dataset over different periods of time and we are entirely missing the data for fiscal 1997, these trends may inaccurately impose unrealistically large differences in country growth rates. Standard errors in all specifications are robust to heteroscedasticity and are clustered by country to control for serial correlation within each country.[15]

---

[15] Bertrand, Duflo, and Mullainathan (2004) discusses how positive serial correlation in outcome, treatment, and control variables can lead to underestimated standard errors on diff-in-diff interaction coefficients. They show that clustering at the group (country in our case, state in theirs) level can alleviate the problem to some extent where there are a large number of groups (such as 50 states, or in our case, 62 countries). Further, while the possibility that our standard errors are underestimated makes it more likely we would find a significant and negative coefficient, it also makes it more likely that we would find a "false" positive interaction coefficient. This makes our result that there are essentially no positive and significant coefficients in our specifications even more striking.

None of these baseline four specifications show a positive and statistically significant interaction term (the "difference-in-differences" coefficient), as would be expected if visa policies were a particularly important contributor to the drop in entries. This is because a positive interaction coefficient would mean that relative to levels before 9/11, countries not requiring visas generally had a larger number of travelers compared to countries that do need visas. If anything, however, the results suggest the opposite. The interaction coefficient is negative in three of the four specifications and significant at the 5 percent level in two of the three. For example, the interaction coefficient in column (1) suggests that, after taking into account country-specific economic variables and other common influences, countries in the visa waiver program typically had a 19 percentage point larger decline in visitors to the United States than countries for which visa policy would be expected to matter. The lone positive interaction coefficient, in column (4), is small quantitatively and highly insignificant. These results imply that changed visa policies were not a particularly important driver of reduced entries, or even that unobserved factors contributing to the drop in travel to the United States are negatively correlated with changes in visa policies. This could be the case, for example, if visa policies were tightened in countries least affected by the increased "fear of flying" after 9/11 that perhaps had a larger impact on potential travelers from advanced economies who did not need a visa to enter the United States.

Other coefficients are consistent with the existing literature on the determinants of travel spending. Stronger growth in each home country is associated with increased travel to the United States, and the elasticity is quite large. The coefficients on the real exchange rate are uniformly negative as expected, implying that a stronger dollar (a real depreciation of the currency of the origin country) leads to less travel to the United States. This is in line with the expectation that a weaker currency in the origin country makes travel to the United States (an import of U.S. services) and the dollar-denominated fee to apply for a visa more expensive for

19

foreigners. The precision of these estimates is substantial, with only one insignificant coefficient across these eight point estimates.

The visa waiver dummy is positive in most specifications, as expected, but is not statistically significant. This is not particularly surprising given it is identified entirely from time series variation in the small number of countries that enter the visa waiver program in the middle of our dataset.

Our results go against the conventional wisdom that post-9/11 changes in visa policy had an important impact on travel to the United States. It should be kept in mind, however that our empirical approach is affected by a number of statistical issues that affect difference-in-differences regression specifications. An ideal setup for such analyses would involve a truly random selection of the "treatment" group—in our case, the group of countries not in the visa waiver program whose travelers were thus affected by changes in visa rules. It is clearly not the case, however, that countries in or out of the visa waiver program are randomly selected. As such, we next add additional conditioning variables as well as run regressions on subsets of the countries to determine the robustness of the lack of a positive and significant interaction coefficient.

We start by adding the real growth in expenditures on travel and tourism by citizens in each of the foreign countries as a new covariate. These data are compiled annually by the World Travel and Tourism Council along with the consulting firm Accenture and include all expenditures by domestic business and pleasure travelers on domestic and foreign travel.[16] We linearly interpolate these annual growth rates and add them to condition on country-specific shocks in demand for any form of travel, not just travel to the United States.[17] As these are

---

[16] We downloaded these data from www.wttc.org.
[17] We are implicitly assuming that the bulk of these travel expenses in all foreign countries is accounted for by travel to domestic and non-U.S. foreign destinations.

growth rates, there are a few substantial outliers, so we drop any country-year observations with a magnitude of change exceeding 20 percent up or down—this screens out about 5 percent of the observations.

Table 4 columns (1) to (4) show results from our original four specifications, modified to include this proxy variable for the overall demand for travel. Though this variable is extrapolated from annual data, while our growth series is extrapolated from quarterly data, one may reasonably be concerned that simultaneous inclusion of both variables gives rise to endogeneity problems. As such, columns (5) to (8) give the results from regressions that include this new travel demand variable but not home country growth. As expected, the variable generally enters with a positive, though typically insignificant, coefficient. Most importantly for our results, however, the interaction coefficients in Table 4 remains negative in most of the specifications (significantly so, in several columns, for at least the 10% level), and is never significant and positive .

Next, we trim the dataset in order to create a more comparable set of countries. For instance, the poorest country in the dataset would be a highly unlikely addition to the visa waiver program in the same way that it would be unusual for the richest country to be excluded. We thus estimate specifications that include only those countries with purchasing-power-parity (PPP) adjusted per capita GDP levels in 2000 ranging from 39 to 66 percent of the per capita GDP of the United States. This includes all countries for which we have data that range in per capita wealth from the Czech Republic to Finland, inclusive. This is among the only ranges in the data where there is a comparable number of visa-waiver and non-visa waiver countries. Table 5 lists the 12 countries falling in this range, organized by membership in the visa waiver program, as well as the regression results for this restricted set. Once again, none of the point estimates on the interaction terms are positive and significant. In fact, all are negative and two are significant at the 10 percent level.

Next, we employ a more formal procedure to achieve the same goal of a more comparable set of visa-waiver and non-visa waiver countries. We generate propensity scores for each country that represent the likelihood that each country would be included in the visa-waiver program based on fixed country characteristics, including the population in 1995, amount of trade with the United States in 1995, PPP-adjusted GDP in 1995, the share of business travelers in 2000, and the natural log of the physical distance from the United States.[18] We then omit from our regressions all countries in the visa waiver program with propensity scores above that of the country outside of the visa waiver program with the highest scores. Similarly, we exclude countries requiring visas that have scores lower than the lowest visa waiver country. This eliminates slightly less than half of the countries in the dataset.

Panel A of Table (6) reports the results from the initial propensity score probit regression. As one might expect, it indicates that countries that are larger, have more trade with the United States, higher per capita GDP, and that are closer to the United States are more likely to be members of the visa waiver program. The probit coefficient on the share of business travelers is insignificant. Panel B gives the list of countries with sufficiently close propensity scores to be kept in the dataset as well as the results from the difference-in-differences regressions we run on this filtered dataset. As was the case with all other specifications, there is again no regression in which the interaction between the 9/11 and visa waiver indicators is positive and significant. Three of the four coefficients are negative, though none of the four is statistically significant.

Having demonstrated the lack of positive and statistically significant impact of changes in visa policy on travel to the United States, we next show in Figure 4 plots of the seasonally adjusted and demeaned time fixed effects when we estimate (1) with no interaction term, and allow for distinct time fixed effects for the visa waiver countries and the non-visa waiver

_____

[18] Log distance was used instead of raw distance in order to satisfy the balancing property in the propensity score

countries. These series were calculated as the residuals of regressions of the actual fixed effects on month dummies and a constant term. Hence, the relative vertical levels of the series have no information, but the time series variation indicates how the seasonally adjusted common component of each group changes over time. As before, this method for seasonal adjustment on a short time-series is somewhat crude and too much emphasis should not be placed on small scale or high frequency movements. Aside from the general upward trends in the lines, one can clearly see sharp drops in the wake of the 9/11 attacks and during the 3 months of major combat operations in Iraq in early 2003.

Panel A of Figure 4 contains our baseline specification where observations from each country are weighted by the level of entrants from that country in 1996. The plot shows that both series had essentially the same long term trend, rising about 30 percent from early 1996 to late 2000 and early 2001. During 2001, before the 9/11 attacks, both series declined somewhat, with the decline in travel by citizens of visa waiver countries somewhat steeper than travel from countries requiring visas. The real plunge in entries in both groups of countries, however, occurs after the 9/11 attacks. Though the gap is not striking relative to differences at other time periods, this plot makes it clear that the visa-waiver countries saw at least as large a negative impact on short-term travel to the United States after 9/11 as the non-visa waiver countries. From levels that look highly similar from early 2000 to late 2001, entries not requiring visas remain persistently far below levels in countries that do need visas. This is what results in the negative interaction term in our difference-in-differences estimates.

6   Caveats

---

regression.

While the previous section provides the most sensible specifications to test the impact of visa policies on overall entries to the United States, several additional caveats to our results should be kept in mind. We have focused on the question of whether visa policy played an important role in the post-9/11 decline in entries, and not on the question of whether changes in visa policy significantly reduced entries for any particular country or resulted in the granting of fewer visas (independent of their use). Our dataset, which measures entrants, is most appropriate for answering this question because it correctly puts more weight on multiple entrants using the same visa, and compared to a dataset purely covering visa issuance, it offers a comparison to similar changes in countries without visa requirements. It does not, however, allow us to study the granting of visas directly (beyond noting that visa rejection rates have not changed significantly).[19]

Our focus on the question of assessing the impact of visa policy on total travel to the United States leads us to emphasize the weighted regressions we have presented as a baseline, attributing more attention to the larger number of visitors from, say, Spain and Chile, than the much smaller number of travelers from, say, Luxembourg or Georgia. Interest in entries from smaller countries, however, might call for greater attention to the unweighted regressions. Panel B of Figure 4 plots the separate time fixed effects for this unweighted case. Differences between the cases in Panel A and B necessarily reflect differences in entry patterns between countries with many entries and countries with few. Indeed, though the two series move largely in parallel from around 2000, the earlier differential trend in the unweighted case suggests that there is a noticeable "visa effect" for some of the smaller countries. In essence, because some small countries, predominantly in the non-visa waiver set, have faster entry growth rates (though the

---

[19] Further, some visas have long lives and hence, some travelers that were previously approved under a cheap visa regime can continue visiting the U.S. after 9/11 without undergoing the new visa procedures. We think this applies to a small number of entrants.

differential trend seems to decline), one might have expected their fixed effect series to rise even further above the visa waiver series in the counterfactual post-9/11 era. The gap, however, remains fairly constant (and shrinks at the end), implying that visa policies may have restricted growth in non-visa waiver program entries from these small countries—travel from these nations was growing rapidly but this was throttled back after 9/11. This dynamic is surely the cause of the positive (though still statistically insignificant) interaction coefficient for the unweighted specification with separate country trends in Table 3.[20] Hence, while we find no meaningful contribution of visa policies to the overall decline in travel to the United States, our analysis does suggest that what would otherwise have been rapid growth in entries from a few small countries was hampered by post-9/11 changes in visa policies.

A final caveat to our results is that we only have data for two years following the 9/11 attacks. The plots in both panels of Figure 4 suggest that the drop in travel by citizens of countries in the visa waiver program abated somewhat toward the end of our dataset. When we run our baseline regression but divide the post-9/11 variable into two separate variables for 2002 and 2003, we find an even more significant difference between the two groups of countries in fiscal year 2002. This further strengthens our result that post-9/11 changes in visa policy do not account for the decline in travel to the United States, since the sharpest decline in fiscal year 2002—just after the attacks—was by travel of people who did not need a visa. This difference is substantially attenuated, though, by the second year after the attacks and its statistical significance is often lost.[21] To be clear, this still means that by the end of fiscal 2003, there was no support for the hypothesis that tighter visa policy reduced travel. If the trend from 2002 to

---

[20] A specification with two different quadratic trends for all of the visa waiver and all of the non-visa waiver countries also results in a positive, though small and statistically insignificant, interaction term. Given the differences between countries even within the two groups, it is more sensible to estimate country-specific rather than group-specific time trends.

[21] These results are available from the authors upon request.

2003 were to continue, however, it is plausible that in later years one might detect an impact of these visa policies on aggregate entries to the United States. Data for arrivals in fiscal years 2004 and beyond would be needed to examine this possibility.

7 Other Factors Influencing Post-9/11 Travel

We have shown that for a wide variety of specifications, and with only a few minor caveats, there is no evidence that entries to the United States of travelers requiring visas dropped by more after 9/11 than travel by people not requiring visas. The evidence suggests that, if there is any difference between the groups, it is that the number of entrants from countries outside of the visa waiver program dropped by less. Since it is implausible that tighter visa policies led to more visitors, we next consider other variables, unrelated to visa policy, that might help explain some of the cross-country variation in the response of potential travelers after the 9/11 attacks.

We start by considering heterogeneity across countries in terms of the composition of travelers between businesspeople and tourists. Our dataset includes an imputed estimate for each country of the number of business travelers as a percent of total non-immigrant entries in 2000. We assume that this composition is relatively stable over time and so include it as an interaction term with the 9/11 indicator that equals zero prior to 9/11 and one after the attacks. In columns (1) to (4) of Table 7, we show the regression results when this business traveler interaction term is included. Since the demand for business travel is likely to be less elastic than pleasure travel, the positive coefficient on this interaction term is unsurprising. As travel became more expensive for everyone after 9/11, business travelers were less likely to respond and change their behavior than tourists were, so that business travel overall declined by less than non-business travel. This estimate is insignificant for the baseline case without country-specific time trends, and does not change the result on the visa waiver interaction term. It does have significant explanatory power for the case with time trends.

Next we consider the impact of different attitudes toward the United States in accounting

for changes in the demand for travel. Ideally, one would like to have a time series show attitudes

before and after 9/11. We do not have such data, but instead must use a snapshot of foreign

views of the United States taken in early 2002 by the Pew Global Attitudes Project. This project

asked citizens of 44 countries about their view of the United States (among many other things).[22]

We assume that the 9/11 attacks did not change the cross-country ordering of views toward the

United States but rather increased the dispersion in such views, so a snapshot of post-9/11 views

would be highly correlated with the change in views from an earlier period. The average survey

response for each country on this question is a number between 1.0 and 4.0, with a score of 3.9,

for instance, representing a case where most recipients held very unfavorable views of the

United States. Unfortunately, the survey data cover only 17 of the countries in our dataset.

Nonetheless, as shown in columns (5) through (8) of Table 7, this interaction coefficient enters

negatively and with a high statistical significance in most of our specifications. The negative

coefficient implies that travelers from countries with a less favorable view of the United States

entered with a lower frequency following the 9/11 attacks compared with before the 9/11 attacks.

This suggests that differing perceptions mattered for travelers' decisions. With only 17 countries

included in the regression, however, we cannot provide more definitive evidence. Further,

inclusion of this variable pushes the 9/11 and visa waiver program interaction coefficient even

further negative, and hence, itself cannot explain the lack of observable "visa effect."

Following on this result, and in light of many articles suggesting that the view of the United

States after 9/11 has worsened in countries with large Muslim communities, we add a variable

that captures the percent of the population that is Muslim in each of the countries in our dataset.

The data are taken from the CIA factbook, available online, which generally provides a specific

---

[22] Specifically, question 61 asks, "Please tell me if you have a very favorable, somewhat favorable, somewhat

percentage for the Muslim population (different types of Muslims, as well as any mention of Islam, were added together for this measure). When it does not, the CIA factbook generally lists several religions as occupying a subset of the population. In these cases, we divide up the residual percentages among the religions mentioned, with slightly higher percentages going to groups listed earlier. For instance, if an entry said "65% Christian, 25% Hindu, others Muslim and Jewish", we allocate the unattributed 10 percent by coding 6 percent as Muslim and 4 percent as Jewish (because Muslim was listed first). In all cases with no mention of Muslims or Islam, we assume their population share is zero.

Columns (1) to (4) of Table 8 show that for every specification, the term capturing the share of Muslim populations interacted with post-9/11 is negative and highly significant. Here it is worth noting that this interaction cannot be a particularly significant quantitative driver of the post-9/11 drop in entries since most of the large countries by entries have small Muslim populations. This coefficient does capture, however, that the few large Muslim countries generally saw relatively large declines in entries, even when compared to similar countries that also required visas. We formalize this by including a triple interaction term in columns (5) to (8), which captures variation by country in or out of the visa-waiver program, after 9/11, by the size of their Muslim population. We do not find any significant results for the triple interaction term. There are few countries in the visa waiver program with substantial Muslim populations, so it is not surprising that we do not find a significant effect. The large unconditional declines from a country like Singapore, though, without the need for visas and with a large Muslim population, suggests that the tendency for countries with large Muslim populations to have less entries after 9/11 is independent of visa policy. As with the "view of U.S." variable, however,

---

unfavorable or very unfavorable opinion of The United States."

accounting for variation in Muslim populations in the data also fails to reverse the sign on the 9/11 and visa waiver program interaction term.

Further discussion of these relationships is outside the scope of our analysis, but we conclude that factors far broader than visa policy, such as whether a traveler is a business or pleasure traveler, or their views of the United States, are more likely to explain the differences across countries in the drop in travel to the United States after 9/11 than changes in visa policy.

8 Conclusion

We find that the decline in visits from countries requiring a visa was not larger than the decline in entries from countries exempt from visa requirements. This suggests that tighter visa policy was not the cause of the sharp drop in business and leisure travel to the United States in the wake of the 9/11 attacks. Changes in the visa process enacted with a delay after 9/11 could be connected with the complaints voiced about visa problems, and these changes perhaps reduced entries somewhat from countries outside the visa waiver program. The timing of this impact, however, does not correspond with the immediate drop in entries, nor does its magnitude stand out when compared with the impact of changes unrelated to visa policy.

We emphasize that our results, taken on their own, do not suggest the correct set of visa policies. Policymakers must jointly weigh the costs and benefits of these policies, while our paper sheds light only on the cost side of this equation. Further, our data only allows us to measure this cost as a function of the number of foreign entries. Hence, our analysis excludes any costs generated by changed visa policies that do not materialize in a forgone visit, such as ill will toward the United States. Several of the groups that have called attention to what they see as a relationship between stricter visa policies and reduced entries offer solutions such as "greeting international travelers with a smile" at airports or improving the efficiency at passport checkpoints in international terminals. Our results do not cast any doubts on efforts such as these, which apply to all entrants regardless of their country of original.

It is difficult to say for sure why the travel plans of people who did not require a visa to visit the United States were affected more (or, at least, not less) after 9/11 than travel by people who needed to obtain a visa. In addition to some of the factors considered in section 7, another explanation for the larger drop in visitors who do not require visas might be connected to the increase in non-monetary costs, such as waiting times and other aggravations associated with increased security involved in traveling to the United States. Before 9/11, short-term visits to the United States were nearly hassle-free for citizens of countries participating in the visa waiver program. In contrast, nationals of other countries, mainly less-developed ones, faced the hazards of the visa application process. After 9/11, visa applicants might well have received greater scrutiny, and indeed, many had to wait longer for visas and travel further for an in-person interview at a U.S. diplomatic post. Travelers who did not require a visa, however, also faced new costs—new hassles, one might say—to enter as a result of post-9/11 changes in security. Compared to the previous near-zero amount of hassle, the added aggravation for travelers from these visa waiver countries was proportionately enormous. While changes in visa policy might have affected travelers needing them, this appears to have been a secondary factor in accounting for the overall decline in short-term business and tourist travel to the United States.

Future research could shed light on the causes of the steep reduction in temporary entries of businesspersons and tourists to the United States after the 9/11 attacks. The results in this paper, however, lead us to dismiss the idea that changes in visa policy are primarily to blame.

References

Clemons, Steven C. (2004). "Land of the Free?" Op-Ed in *The New York Times*, March 31. ("United States Visa Application Rejection Rates" found at http://www.steveclemons.com/visafees.htm, June 15, 2004.)

Bureau of Consular Affairs, Department of State (2004). "Initiatives by the Bureau of Consular Affairs to Enhance National Security -- Fact Sheet, September 5, 2002" found at http://www.state.gov/coalition/cr/fs/13316.htm, May 3, 2004.

Office of Immigration Statistics, Department of Homeland Security (2004, 2005). *Yearbook of Immigration Statistics*.

Office of the Inspector General, Department of State (2004). "Review of Nonimmigrant Visa Issuance Policy and Procedures (ISP-I-03-26)" found at http://oig.state.gov/oig/lbry/isprpts/domestic/26634.htm, May 3, 2004.

Di Matteo, Livio. (1993). "Determinants of cross-border trips and spending by Canadians in the United States." *Canadian Business Economics*.

Bertrand, Duflo, Mullainaithan (2004). "How much should we trust Differences-in-Differences Estimates?" *Quarterly Journal of Economics*.

General Accounting Office, United States (2002). "Visa Process Should be Strengthened as an Antiterrorism Tool." October.

General Accounting Office, United States (2002). "Implications of Eliminating the Visa Waiver Program." GAO-03-38. November.

Gray, Peter H. (1966). "The Demand for International Travel by the United States and Canada." *International Economics Review*.

Kwack, Sung Y. (1971). "Effects of Income and Prices on Travel Spending Abroad, 1960 III-1967 IV." *International Economics Review*.

Orrenius, Pia M. (2003). "U.S. Immigration and Economic Growth: Putting Policy on Hold," *Southwest Economy*, Federal Reserve Bank of Dallas, November/December.

Passel, Jeffrey S. (2005). "Unauthorized Migrants: Numbers and Characteristics", *Pew Hispanic Center White Paper*, June 14.

Rhomberg, R.R. and L. Boissonneault (1964). "Effects of income and price changes on the U.S. balance of payments," *IMF Staff Papers*.

Rose, Thom J. (2004). "U.S. visas: Applications down, prices up." *United Press International*. April 15.

Siskin, Alison (2004). "Visa Waiver Program." CRS Report for Congress, December.

Vilasuso, Jon and Fredric C. Menz. (1998). "Domestic Price, (Expected) Foreign Price, and Travel Spending by Canadians in the United States." *The Canadian Journal of Economics*.

Table 1: Participation in the Visa Waiver Program

	Country	Date of Inclusion		Date of Removal	
		Month	Year	Month	Year
(1)	United Kingdom	July	1988		
(2)	Japan	December	1988		
(3)	France	July	1989		
(4)	Switzerland	July	1989		
(5)	Germany	July	1989		
(6)	Sweden	July	1989		
(7)	Italy	July	1989		
(8)	Netherlands	July	1989		
(9)	Andorra	October	1991		
(10)	Austria	October	1991		
(11)	Belgium	October	1991		
(12)	Denmark	October	1991		
(13)	Finland	October	1991		
(14)	Iceland	October	1991		
(15)	Lichtenstein	October	1991		
(16)	Luxembourg	October	1991		
(17)	Monaco	October	1991		
(18)	New Zealand	October	1991		
(19)	Norway	October	1991		
(20)	San Marino	October	1991		
(21)	Spain	October	1991		
(22)	Brunei	July	1993		
(23)	Ireland	April	1995		
(24)	Argentina	July	1996	February	2002
(25)	Australia	July	1996		
(26)	Slovenia	September	1997		
(27)	Portugal	August	1999		
(28)	Singapore	August	1999		
(29)	Uruguay	August	1999	April	2003

Table 2: Summary Statistics of Non-immigrant Entries in the Sample

		Number of Countries	Number of Non-Immigrant Entries		Decline
			Fiscal Year 2000	Fiscal Year 2003	
	Aggregate Data	204	34,113,528	28,214,826	-17%
	Full Sample	65	28,953,399	24,158,712	-17%
	Visa-Waiver Eligible and Canada	**22**	**18,896,232**	**14,805,762**	**-22%**
(1)	Australia		593,246	552,916	-7%
(2)	Austria		213,384	131,340	-38%
(3)	Belgium		258,904	179,559	-31%
(4)	Denmark		178,349	163,408	-8%
(5)	Finland		118,369	86,742	-27%
(6)	France		1,329,169	1,040,949	-22%
(7)	Germany		2,146,442	1,444,665	-33%
(8)	Iceland		31,803	25,229	-21%
(9)	Ireland		405,583	372,137	-8%
(10)	Italy		810,613	641,216	-21%
(11)	Japan		5,259,703	3,593,469	-32%
(12)	Luxembourg		12,913	7,640	-41%
(13)	Netherlands		684,041	546,191	-20%
(14)	New Zealand		200,147	204,219	2%
(15)	Norway		166,300	142,935	-14%
(16)	Portugal		114,701	84,436	-26%
(17)	Singapore		119,632	81,919	-32%
(18)	Slovenia		18,035	11,732	-35%
(19)	Spain		466,168	430,070	-8%
(20)	Sweden		377,000	257,899	-32%
(21)	Switzerland		390,237	257,898	-34%
(22)	United Kingdom		5,001,493	4,549,193	-9%
	Non Visa-Waiver Eligible	**40**	**5,043,926**	**4,506,576**	**-11%**
(1)	Belize	30859	30,859	26,587	-14%
(2)	Botswana	2392	2,392	1,945	-19%
(3)	Chile	211738	211,738	140,553	-34%
(4)	Colombia	478142	478,142	389,768	-18%
(5)	Costa Rica	173112	173,112	149,998	-13%
(6)	Croatia	24925	24,925	19,960	-20%
(7)	Cyprus	13345	13,345	9,554	-28%
(8)	Czech Republic	52910	52,910	44,478	-16%
(9)	Ecuador	138661	138,661	163,531	18%
(10)	Estonia	8856	8,856	8,758	-1%
(11)	Greece	79359	79,359	60,083	-24%
(12)	Georgia	4869	4,869	5,290	9%
(13)	Guatemala	183162	183,162	189,989	4%
(14)	Hong Kong	129401	129,401	75,780	-41%
(15)	Hungary	68696	68,969	45,020	-35%
(16)	India	560110	560,110	559,805	0%
(17)	Indonesia	97249	97,247	65,071	-33%
(18)	Iran	28425	28,425	10,398	-63%
(19)	Israel	357644	357,644	307,101	-14%
(20)	Jamaica	277895	277,895	224,478	-19%
(21)	Jordan	30631	30,631	21,214	-31%
(22)	Korea	811951	811,951	845,272	4%
(23)	Kyrgyzstan	2000	2,000	1,668	-17%
(24)	Latvia	11733	11,733	10,494	-11%
(25)	Lithuania	13747	13,747	15,811	15%
(26)	Macau	1439	1,439	937	-35%
(27)	Malaysia	95709	95,709	53,160	-44%
(28)	Malta	9112	9,112	5,790	-36%
(29)	Mauritius	3028	3,028	1,415	-53%
(4)	Morocco	27590	27,590	18,021	-35%
(5)	Peru	229307	229,307	224,542	-2%
(6)	Philippines	281463	281,463	273,439	-3%
(7)	Poland	147125	147,125	155,810	6%
(8)	Romania	44162	44,162	49,722	13%
(9)	Slovak Republic	20933	20,933	24,629	18%
(10)	South Africa	132818	132,818	108,232	-19%
(11)	Sri Lanka	17656	17,656	13,846	-22%
(12)	Thailand	97560	97,560	74,195	-24%
(13)	Tunisia	12885	12,885	4,181	-68%
(14)	Turkey	131056	131,056	106,051	-19%
	Excluded	**3**	**5,013,241**	**4,846,374**	**-3%**
(1)	Argentina		548,798	244,477	-55%
(2)	Canada		260,086	243,755	-6%
(3)	Mexico	4204357	4,204,357	4,358,142	4%

Table 3: Baseline Specification Regression Results

	Log Entrants			
	(1)	(2)	(3)	(4)
Post-9/11 * Visa Waiver Program	-0.186 (0.091)**	-0.113 (0.055)**	-0.086 (0.084)	0.037 (0.053)
VWP	0.097 (0.077)	0.497 (0.470)	-0.005 (0.053)	0.716 (0.590)
Real GDP Growth in Home Country	0.675 (0.499)	0.951 (0.290)***	0.977 (0.321)***	0.911 (0.226)***
Real Exchange Rate Growth	-0.243 (0.081)***	-0.206 (0.086)**	-0.259 (0.049)***	-0.156 (0.057)***
Separate Time Trends	N	N	Y	Y
Weighted	Y	N	Y	N
Fixed Effects	Time Country	Time Country	Time Country	Time Country
Excluded Countries	Canada Mexico Argentina	Canada Mexico Argentina	Canada Mexico Argentina	Canada Mexico Argentina
Countries	62	62	62	62
Observations	4604	4604	4604	4604

* Significant at 10%, ** Significant at 5%, *** Significant at 1%

Notes: Standard errors are robust to general heteroskedasticity and are clustered by country to account for serial correlation.

Table 4: Results Conditional on Domestic Demand

	Log Entrants							
	(1)	(2)	(3)	(4)	(5)	(6)	(7)	(8)
Post-9/11 * Visa Waiver Program	-0.172 (0.087)*	-0.091 (0.056)	-0.078 (0.081)	0.044 (0.057)	-0.187 (0.084)**	-0.102 (0.060)*	-0.077 (0.071)	0.035 (0.064)
Real Growth in Home Travel Expenditures	0.498 (0.412)	0.137 (0.200)	0.682 (0.335)**	-0.090 (0.222)	0.538 (0.406)	0.310 (0.179)*	0.769 (0.325)**	0.136 (0.205)
VWP	0.097 (0.082)	0.536 (0.498)	-0.025 (0.042)	0.780 (0.634)	0.082 (0.083)	0.510 (0.501)	-0.021 (0.041)	0.776 (0.640)
Real GDP Growth in Home Country	0.351 (0.408)	1.046 (0.296)***	0.557 (0.193)***	1.044 (0.241)***				
Real Exchange Rate Growth	-0.253 (0.092)***	-0.169 (0.053)***	-0.279 (0.054)***	-0.145 (0.036)***	-0.264 (0.080)***	-0.228 (0.048)***	-0.302 (0.055)***	-0.208 (0.041)***
Separate Time Trends	N	N	Y	Y	N	N	Y	Y
Weighted	Y	N	Y	N	Y	N	Y	N
Fixed Effects	Time Country	Time Country	Time Country	Time Country	Time Country	Time Country	Time Country	Time Country
Excluded Countries	Canada Mexico Argentina	Canada Mexico Argentina	Canada Mexico Argentina	Canada Mexico Argentina	Canada Mexico Argentina	Canada Mexico Argentina	Canada Mexico Argentina	Canada Mexico Argentina
Countries	59	59	59	59	59	59	59	59
Observations	4223	4223	4223	4223	4223	4223	4223	4223

* Significant at 10%, ** Significant at 5%, *** Significant at 1%

Notes: Standard errors are robust to general heteroskedasticity and are clustered by country to account for serial correlation.

Table 5: Results Conditional on Country GDP

VWP	Non-VWP
Portugal	Czech Republic
Slovenia	Greece
Spain	Mauritius
New Zealand	Korea
Italy	Malta
	Cyprus
	Israel

		Log Entrants			
		(1)	(2)	(3)	(4)
Post-9/11 * Visa Waiver Program		-0.160 (0.081)*	-0.017 (0.117)	-0.179 (0.089)*	-0.038 (0.183)
VWP		0.162 (0.072)**	0.978 (0.878)	0.138 (0.099)	1.412 (0.939)
Real GDP Growth in Home Country		2.753 (1.054)**	3.271 (1.826)	2.725 (0.901)**	2.566 (1.502)
Real Exchange Rate Growth		0.084 (0.201)	0.188 (0.253)	0.064 (0.179)	0.061 (0.265)
Separate Time Trends		N	N	Y	Y
Weighted		Y	N	Y	N
Fixed Effects		Time Country	Time Country	Time Country	Time Country
Countries		12	12	12	12
Observations		940	940	940	940

* Significant at 10%, ** Significant at 5%, *** Significant at 1%

Notes: Standard errors are robust to general heteroskedasticity and are clustered by country to account for serial correlation.

Table 6: Regression Results Conditional on Propensity Score

Panel A: Propensity Score Determination (Probit)

Propensity Score Probit	Coefficient	Std. Error
Population 1995	5.61E-04	1.98E-04
Trade 1995	1.06E-08	1.45E-09
PPP-relative GDP 1995	5.27E-02	9.70E-04
Business share 2000	3.13E-01	2.81E-01
Ln_Distance	-2.32E-01	3.71E-02

Panel B: Regression Results from Propensity-Score Restricted Dataset

VWP	Non-VWP		Log Entrants			
			(1)	(2)	(3)	(4)
Australia	Botswana					
Austria	Chile	Post-9/11 * Visa	-0.086	-0.024	-0.136	0.078
Belgium	Croatia	Waiver Program	(0.117)	(0.066)	(0.098)	(0.053)
Denmark	Cyprus					
Finland	Czech Republic	VWP	0.067	0.058	-0.070	0.001
France	Estonia		(0.076)	(0.047)	(0.051)	(0.078)
Germany	Georgia					
Iceland	Greece	Real GDP Growth	1.783	0.955	1.598	0.852
Ireland	Hong Kong	in Home Country	(0.708)**	(0.364)**	(0.581)	(0.341)**
Italy	Israel					
Netherlands	Korea	Real Exchange	-0.042	0.069	-0.130	0.103
New Zealand	Kyrgzstan	Rate Growth	(0.136)	(0.219)	(0.060)	(0.198)
Norway	Latvia					
Portugal	Lithuania	Separate Time Trends	N	N	Y	Y
Spain	Macau					
Sweden	Malta	Weighted	Y	N	Y	N
United Kingdom	Mauritius					
	Slovak Republic	Fixed Effects	Time Country	Time Country	Time Country	Time Country
		Countries	35	35	35	35
		Observations	2736	2736	2736	2736

* Significant at 10%, ** Significant at 5%, *** Significant at 1%

Notes: Standard errors are robust to general heteroskedasticity and are clustered by country to account for serial correlation.

Table 7: Regression Results Conditional on Business Travelers and View of U.S.

				Log Entrants				
	(1)	(2)	(3)	(4)	(5)	(6)	(7)	(8)
Post-9/11 * Visa Waiver Program	-0.118 (0.084)	-0.109 (0.054)**	-0.036 (0.066)	0.045 (0.053)	-0.378 (0.098)	-0.262 (0.072)***	-0.202 (0.108)*	-0.031 (0.070)
Post-9/11 * Share of Business Travelers	0.747 (0.518)	0.314 (0.511)	0.569 (0.255)**	0.769 (0.354)**				
Post-9/11 * View of U.S.					-0.537 (0.251)**	-0.205 (0.063)***	-0.094 (0.141)	-0.219 (0.058)***
VWP	0.060 (0.076)	0.489 (0.474)	0.014 (0.058)	0.726 (0.589)				
Real GDP Growth in Home Country	0.899 (0.402)**	0.965 (0.277)	1.058 (0.327)***	0.927 (0.217)***	0.626 -0.685	0.307 (0.367)	1.158 (0.413)**	1.026 (0.321)***
Real Exchange Rate Growth	-0.172 (0.070)**	-0.196 (0.079)	-0.215 (0.037)***	-0.147 (0.052)***	-0.257 (0.077)***	-0.147 (0.034)***	-0.281 (0.071)***	-0.150 (0.036)***
Separate Time Trends	N	N	Y	Y	N	N	Y	Y
Weighted	Y	N	Y	N	Y	N	Y	N
Fixed Effects	Time Country	Time Country	Time Country	Time Country	Time Country	Time Country	Time Country	Time Country
Excluded Countries	Canada Mexico Argentina	Canada Mexico Argentina	Canada Mexico Argentina	Canada Mexico Argentina	Canada Mexico Argentina	Canada Mexico Argentina	Canada Mexico Argentina	Canada Mexico Argentina
Countries	62	59	59	59	17	17	17	17
Observations	4604	4223	4223	4223	1316	1316	1316	1316

* Significant at 10%, ** Significant at 5%, *** Significant at 1%

Notes: Standard errors are robust to general heteroskedasticity and are clustered by country to account for serial correlation.

Table 8: Regression Results Conditional on Muslim Population

				Log Entrants				
	(1)	(2)	(3)	(4)	(5)	(6)	(7)	(8)
Post-9/11 * Visa Waiver Program	-0.211 (0.092)**	-0.156 (0.058)***	-0.119 (0.083)	-0.010 (0.053)	-0.214 (0.093)**	-0.122 (0.059)**	-0.125 (0.085)	-0.023 (0.066)
Post-9/11 * Share of Muslims in the Population	-0.255 (0.127)**	-0.255 (0.093)***	-0.370 (0.103)***	-0.268 (0.055)***	-0.264 (0.121)**	-0.233 (0.092)**	-0.387 (0.106)***	-0.276 (0.055)***
Post-9/11 * Visa Waiver Program * Share of Muslims in the Population					0.184 (1.134)	-1.338 (0.744)	0.322 (0.441)	0.448 (0.653)
VWP	0.106 (0.075)	0.507 (0.468)	-0.008 (0.049)	0.713 (0.592)	0.100 (0.083)	0.552 (0.480)	-0.006 (0.053)	0.718 (0.595)
Real GDP Growth in Home Country	0.633 (0.534)	1.012 (0.286)***	0.969 (0.325)***	0.938 (0.212)***	0.693 (0.488)	0.990 (0.279)***	0.975 (0.324)***	0.938 (0.211)***
Real Exchange Rate Growth	-0.244 (0.081)***	-0.162 (0.063)**	-0.256 (0.052)***	-0.125 (0.049)**	-0.242 (0.080)***	-0.159 (0.067)**	-0.254 (0.049)***	-0.126 (0.048)
Separate Time Trends	N	N	Y	Y	N	N	Y	Y
Weighted	Y	N	Y	N	Y	N	Y	N
Fixed Effects	Time Country	Time Country	Time Country	Time Country	Time Country	Time Country	Time Country	Time Country
Excluded Countries	Canada Mexico Argentina	Canada Mexico Argentina	Canada Mexico Argentina	Canada Mexico Argentina	Canada Mexico Argentina	Canada Mexico Argentina	Canada Mexico Argentina	Canada Mexico Argentina
Countries	62	62	62	62	62	62	62	62
Observations	4606	4606	4606	4606	4606	4606	4606	4606

* Significant at 10%, ** Significant at 5%, *** Significant at 1%

Notes: Standard errors are robust to general heteroskedasticity and are clustered by country to account for serial correlation.

Figure 1: Non-Immigrant Entries

Panel A: Annual Non-Immigrant Entries (Published)

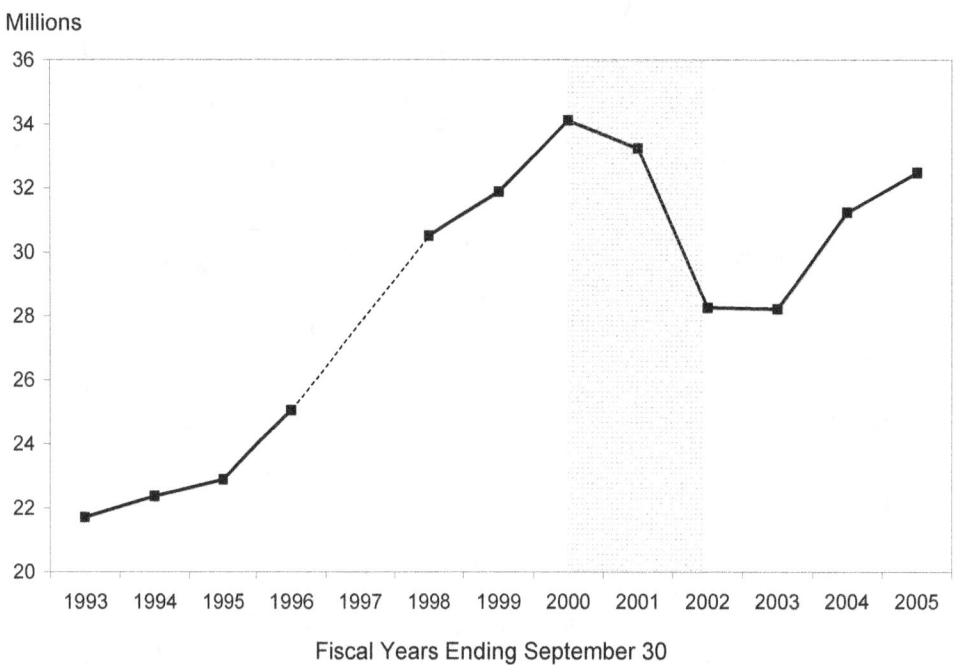

Fiscal Years Ending September 30

Panel B: Monthly Non-Immigrant Entries (Our Dataset)

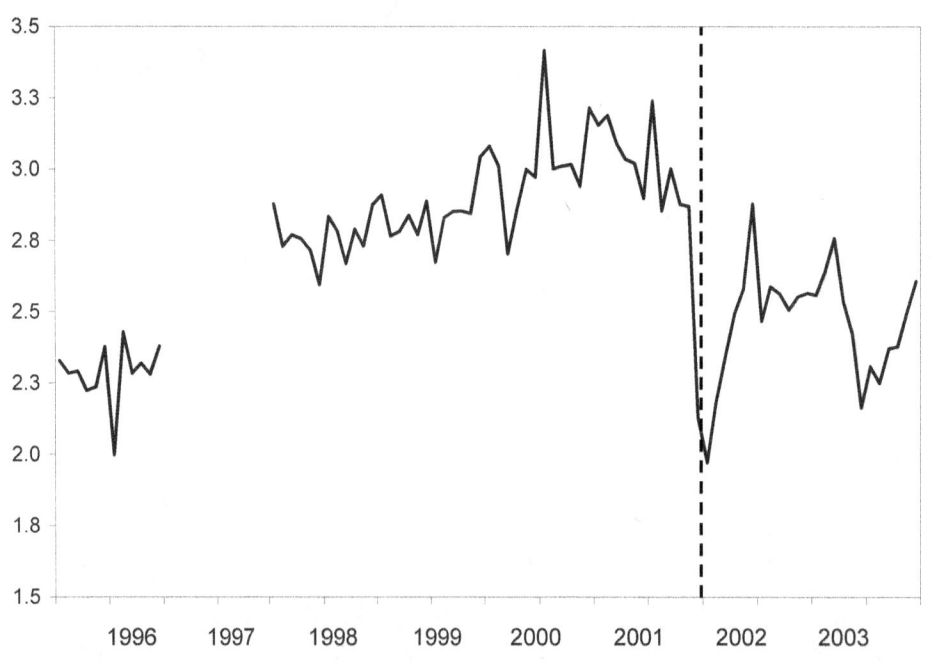

Figure 2: Passengers on U.S. Domestic Non-Stop Segments

U.S. Domestic Non-Stop Passenger Emplanements, Millions

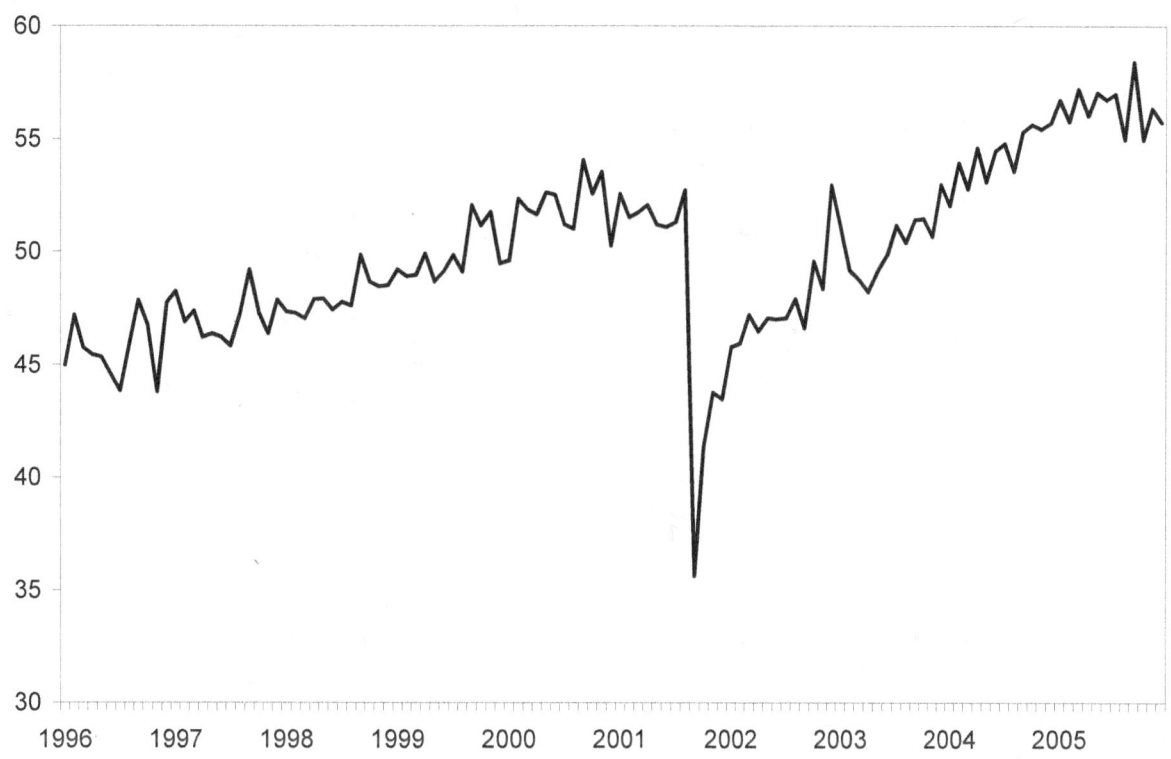

Source: Bureau of Transportation Statistics, U.S. Department of Transportation

Figure 3: Monthly Non-Immigrant Entries, by Participation in the Visa Waiver Program

Panel A: Levels

Millions (Seasonally Adjusted Monthly Data)

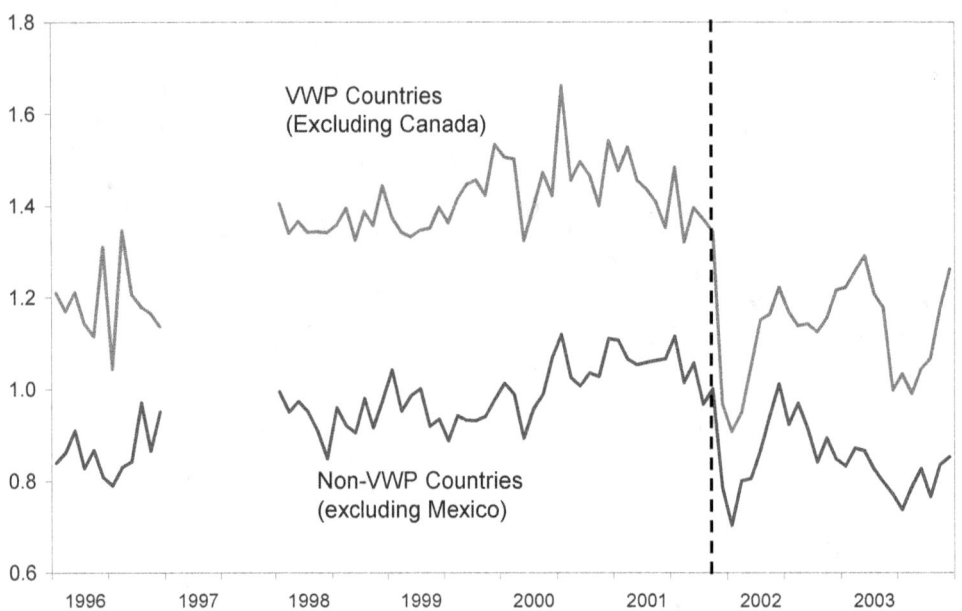

Note: Constant panel from our dataset, excludes Argen ina, Australia, Portugal, Singapore, Slovenia, and Uruguay

Panel B: Natural Log Levels

Natural Log Levels (Seasonally Adjusted Monthly Data)

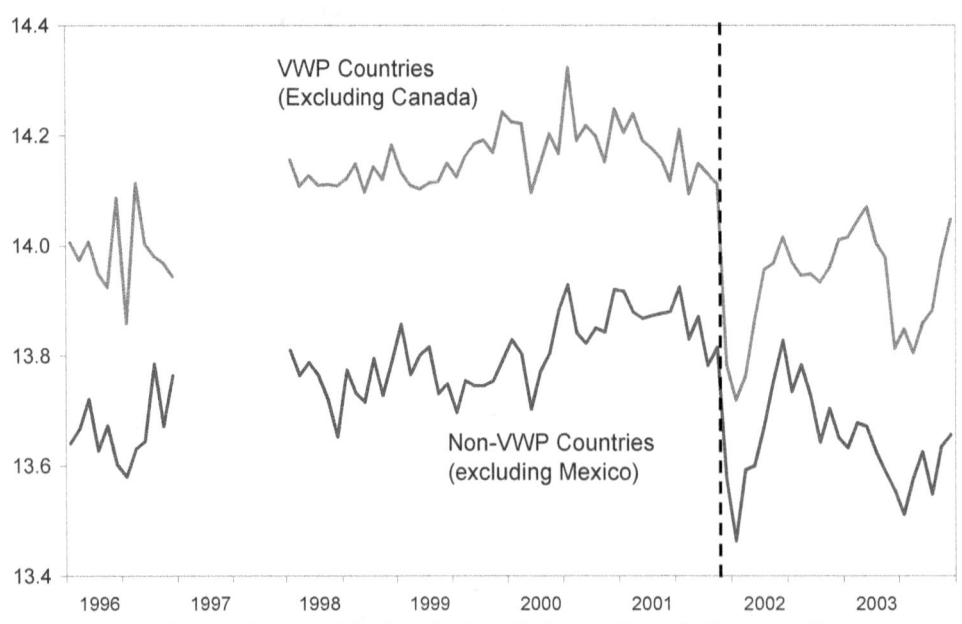

Note: Constant panel from our dataset, excludes Argentina, Australia, Portugal, Singapore, Slovenia, and Uruguay

Figure 4: Separate Time Fixed Effects

Panel A: Separate Time Fixed Effects, Baseline Case (Weighted)

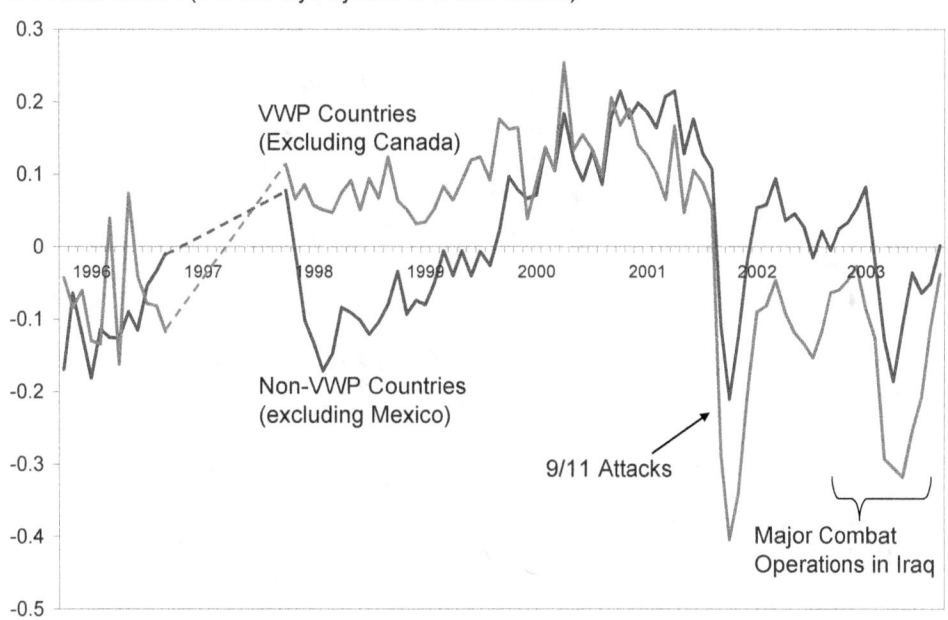

Panel B: Separate Time Fixed Effects (Unweighted)

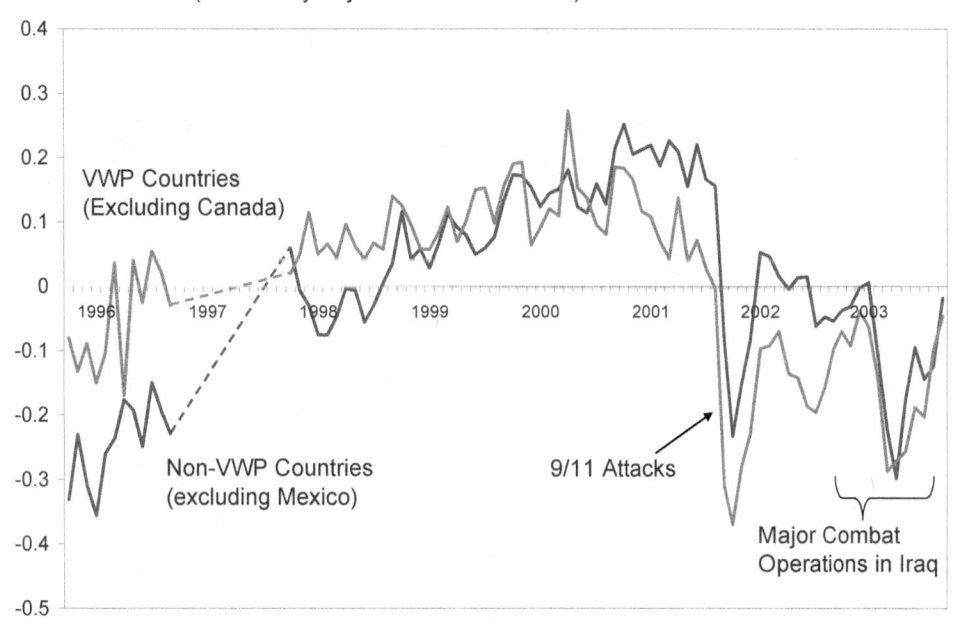

Table A1: Regression Results For Various Data Samples

	Log Entrants											
	(1)	(2)	(3)	(4)	(5)	(6)	(7)	(8)	(9)	(10)	(11)	(12)
Post-9/11 * Visa Waiver Program	-0.247 (0.111)**	-0.100 (0.058)*	0.013 (0.097)	0.018 (0.072)	-0.275 (0.105)**	-0.105 (0.058)*	-0.009 (0.095)	0.039 (0.052)	-0.155 (0.098)	-0.109 (0.054)**	-0.061 (0.086)	0.015 (0.075)
VWP	0.277 (0.128)**	0.447 (0.350)	0.185 (0.097)	0.508 (0.347)	0.054 (0.084)	0.472 (0.468)	-0.020 (0.066)	0.712 (0.586)	0.273 (0.105)**	0.466 (0.352)	0.222 (0.100)**	0.514 (0.348)
Real GDP Growth in Home Country	0.634 (0.355)*	0.920 (0.271)***	0.989 (0.435)**	-0.128 (0.230)***	0.762 (0.414)*	0.965 (0.285)***	1.312 (0.365)***	0.953 (0.224)***	0.560 (0.417)	0.899 (0.274)***	0.650 (0.372)*	0.842 (0.232)***
Real Exchange Rate Growth	-0.278 (0.058)***	-0.195 (0.087)**	-0.235 (0.050)***	-0.128 (0.067)*	-0.219 (0.059)***	-0.197 (0.089)**	-0.241 (0.048)***	-0.157 (0.054)***	-0.289 (0.069)***	-0.202 (0.085)**	-0.258 (0.049)***	-0.127 (0.069)*
Separate Time Trends	N	N	Y	Y	N	N	Y	Y	N	N	Y	Y
Weighted	Y	N	Y	N	Y	N	Y	N	Y	N	Y	N
Fixed Effects	Time Country	Time Country	Time Country	Time Country	Time Country	Time Country	Time Country	Time Country	Time Country	Time Country	Time Country	Time Country
Excluded Countries	None	None	None	None	Argentina	Argentina	Argentina	Argentina	Canada Mexico	Canada Mexico	Canada Mexico	Canada Mexico
Countries	65	65	65	65	64	64	64	64	63	63	63	63
Observations	4856	4856	4856	4856	4772	4772	4772	4772	4688	4688	4688	4688

* Significant at 10%, ** Significant at 5%, *** Significant at 1%

Notes: Standard errors are robust to general heteroskedasticity and are clustered by country to account for serial correlation.

44

Table A2: Regression Results For Various Weighting Schemes

	Log Entrants					
	(1)	(2)	(3)	(4)	(5)	(6)
Post-9/11 * Visa Waiver Program	-0.060 (0.065)	0.066 (0.050)	-0.247 (0.080)***	0.080 (0.050)*	-0.134 (0.106)	-0.079 (0.091)
VWP	0.419 (0.383)	0.561 (0.489)	0.165 (0.153)	0.169 (0.203)	0.081 (0.058)	0.087 (0.045)*
Real GDP Growth in Home Country	1.022 (0.337)***	1.040 (0.242)***	0.069 (0.249)	0.958 (0.201)***	0.995 (0.290)***	1.282 (0.212)***
Real Exchange Rate Growth	-0.246 (0.068)***	-0.161 (0.056)***	-0.246 (0.090)***	-0.191 (0.028)***	-0.303 (0.081)***	-0.292 (0.068)***
Separate Time Trends	N	Y	N	Y	N	Y
Weighting Variable (All from 1995)	Per-Capita GDP	Per-Capita GDP	Population	Population	Bilateral Trade (USD)	Bilateral Trade (USD)
Fixed Effects	Time Country	Time Country	Time Country	Time Country	Time Country	Time Country
Excluded Countries	Canada Mexico Argentina	Canada Mexico Argentina	Canada Mexico Argentina	Canada Mexico Argentina	Canada Mexico Argentina Luxembourg# Botswana#	Canada Mexico Argentina Luxembourg# Botswana#
Countries	62	62	62	62	60	60
Observations	4604	4604	4604	4604	4452	4452

* Significant at 10%, ** Significant at 5%, *** Significant at 1%
# Missing 1995 Trade Data

Notes: Standard errors are robust to general heteroskedasticity and are clustered by country to account for serial correlation.

www.ingramcontent.com/pod-product-compliance
Lightning Source LLC
Chambersburg PA
CBHW052019280526
45793CB00005B/1038